ONE STEP CLOSER TO MORE!

From Clicks to Cash Flow

Charles Blair "The Mad Scientist"

Table of Contents

Who Am I?

I'm Charles Blair, "The Mad Scientist".

I am a published author, national speaker, and consultant. I am widely considered one of the nation's top internet marketing experts. My insight and ability to apply cutting edge marketing strategies, client attraction techniques, and lead generation, have made me a highly sought after consultant and speaker. My skills are exhibited at internet, social marketing, and real estate investing seminars across the country.

I have an extensive list of clients that are considered a virtual "who's who" in the industry, such as: Than

Merrill, Kenny Rushing, Alan Cowgill, Guy Cook, Juan Zayas, Allen Chaney, Marcel Humphrey, Al Aiello, Mark Whitten, Valarie Scott, and countless other business owners and entrepreneurs across the country.

I have spoken nationwide, educating and entertaining audiences at the All Things Google Summit, Hype Free Seminars, The Tampa Bay Business Owners' Association, National Real Estate Investors Association, and The Speakers Academy. I have been both a host and a guest on a number of radio programs and featured in the Baltimore Sun.

Although born and raised in the projects of east Baltimore and a junior high school dropout, I have proven to be a survivor in any environment. I gained quick success in real estate investing, completing over 300 deals and became the largest minority owner of real estate in downtown Baltimore. I am the owner and founder of Page One Success, a leading online business marketing and design company.

I'm writing this book to show you how I have used the same skills, tools and insights used by internet marketers to experience success with my and my client's businesses.

Chapter 1: Google Domination

Google is the number one search engine in the world. Most countries have some form of Google that will give search results in their native language. Nowadays the term "Google It" is synonymous for looking something up online whether you're using Google or not. It has become a part of pop culture as well as an integral part of the way we use the internet.

There are over 5 billion searches done on Google a day. To be more exact, there are 5,134,000,000 according to the latest statistics shared by Google.

Let's stop and think about that for a second.

There are over 7 billion people in the world. There are almost as many Google searches being done a day as there are people in the world.

But out of those 5 billion searches, 89% don't click past the first page of search results. That means if your website isn't showing up on the first page of Google searches, you're not really gaining access to the people doing all of those searches.

Your website NEEDS to be on the first page of Google.

How to Get on the First Page of Google

The first thing you've got to remember is that Google is a search engine that thrives off of high quality information. It uses these things called bots or web crawlers that go out to the web every day and look for new information.

The bots (as I will call them for the rest of the book), are programmed to recognize fresh, original content which is why you must always work to consistently create new content and share it regularly. I'm going to go into how you can do that later in this book.

The main thing to remember is to consistently provide value with your website, and you will be on the right path to staying well ranked in Google and appearing on the first page of search results. However, there are some specific things you need to do to ensure that you are able to not only outrank your competition but appear "above the fold" in Google search results.

Wait, what does "above the fold" mean?

This is an important internet marketing term. It simply means that your website will appear towards the top of the web page before you have to scroll down. This is a very simple concept that many people forget about when creating their business website. Let me show you what I mean.

Here is the main page of one of my company websites:

As you can tell, there is more information on this page but in order to see it, you have to scroll down. All of the information in this picture is considered "above the fold". Think about what would happen if you didn't have a chance to scroll down.

The only information you would have about my company is what you see in Figure 1-1. But if you notice, there is a lot of great information there that will answer a lot of questions you may have while highlighting some of the different things my company is offering.

When your website appears in search results, it's most ideal if it appears "above the fold". This is the most ideal position because it puts your website in the position to gain a lot of exposure when it pops up in Google search.

There are different factors that you must consider when putting together your website to ensure that you appear on the first page of Google searches.

1. Quality Content is Key

   Remember when I said that your website must provide value? This is how you do it. Google really wants to make sure that the search engine is providing high quality, top notch information to the people that have come to rely on it for a great deal of the information they find online. By focusing on providing quality in everything that you do, you are playing right into what Google wants which will always work in your favor.

   Quality content is typically original, informative and insightful. You can't go out and rehash what someone else has already covered and expect that to be enough. Your website is a digital representation of your business. If the content looks thrown together and not well thought out, people will assume the same of your business.

Take the time to put the effort into what your website is saying. Not only will people decide whether your business is providing value based on the content, so will Google. If Google decides your content is low quality, you won't receive the exposure you need to be successful online.

2. Keywords, Keywords, Keywords

Keywords are how people search for things online. They type in what they're looking for and browse the search results until they find it. You have to make sure the keywords you use are the same ones your clients are searching for online. Keywords are going to continually come up throughout this book so it's important that you recognize their value. You want to the keywords that you'd like to rank for and include them on your website.

Here are some places that you should make sure to add your keywords:

a. Website Titles

There is title text throughout your website. It's typically the text that is in the header of a section or page. Your website titles must include some form of a desired keyword in it. If you want your website to rank well for the different products and services, they should be included in the titles. If you have one or two main keywords you'd like to rank for, they should be used a few times in the different title text. Don't overdo it though. You need your website to be readable and make sense to the visitors that are browsing it but the keywords should be present.

b. Video Titles

When you create the title of the videos that you're going to be sharing on YouTube (more about that later), you should include the main keyword you want your website to rank for. Those titles will come up in Google searches so you want to make sure there are keywords in them.

c. Blog Posts

Your blog post titles should be as keyword friendly as possible. Not only will they come up in search results, but people should be able to easily tell what each post is about when they visit your website. Since you are providing valuable information, you want people to be able to get what need with relative ease.

d. File names

When you create videos, images and other files that you share online, those names should include keywords. When the bots crawl your website looking for content, they look everywhere. They search the text that you're sharing as well as the names of the files you have on your website. This is a secret tip that pro internet marketers use to their advantage. The easiest way to do this is by using the same title you would on the website, video or blog post in the name of the file.

3. Consistent Updates

   You can't put up a great website and walk away from it. Gone are the days when your website is essentially a digital brochure for your business. Your website is a living, breathing organism that must be fed, updated and pruned consistently. Don't get me wrong. I'm not suggesting that you constantly redo your website. That would be way too much work and is unnecessary.

   The key is to find a way to consistently update the content on your website to keep visitors coming back and the bots happy. You can do this by sharing articles, blog posts and/or videos on your website. This doesn't have to be time consuming. You can focus on short snippets of high value information rather than long drawn out descriptions and explanations.

   Don't stress yourself out by trying to post something new every day. You can add new content 2-3 times a week and that will still be very effective. Your website shouldn't be a source of stress. It's there to enhance your business, not take away from it. It is a valuable marketing tool but if you make room in your schedule, you can still share consistent updates.

Now that you have some idea of what is necessary to rank high in Google search results, let's dive into the nitty gritty of it all. I want to give you some specific insights you can easily put into practice.

Google has three metrics that it uses to determine where to place websites:

- Organic Search Results (free traffic)
- Google Places
- Paid Search Results (Pay Per Click or PPC)

Let's get into what each one of these metrics mean and how they can help you.

Organic Search Results

When someone finds your website by means of a keyword based search, it's called an organic search. That means you didn't do any type of specific thing to lead them to your website. They didn't click a link in your email signature or on your social media profile. In a nutshell, this is any type of search results where the person doesn't type your web address in the browser search or click on your web address looking for your website.

This is the most valuable type of search results and the ones you are working to rank well for by using keywords. I know I mentioned previously that you need to know what words your customers are searching. But you don't have to worry about sneaking into anyone's house and look over their shoulder while they do web searches to do that. Google has some great tools that give you a glimpse into the mind of your customers.

Google Adwords

This is the program that Google created to make it possible for businesses to advertise on Google. It allows you to create keyword based ads that come up in relevant Google searches. This is a free program to join and there are a lot of features you can take advantage of without paying for any advertising.

Keyword Planner

The keyword planner is a free tool that lets you search for keywords to see how often they're searched and how that affects their value. You have access to this tool as soon as you create a Google Adwords account. It allows you to essentially read the minds of buyers, sellers and renters that are searching online.

There was a time when buying, selling or renting real estate happened largely in person. Unless someone was a licensed real estate professional, they often didn't have access to any of the databases and information used to research properties. Now a lot of that information is available online so people tend to start their search there before reaching out to a professional.

Actually, 90% of your prospects are going to look online for what they want first. If you can get your website in front of those people, you increase the chances that they call you when they're ready to start the process of buying, selling or renting. The keyword planner will help you determine which keywords are being most commonly used when your customers do their online research.

Here are the steps you should follow to identify those words:

1. Sign up for Google Adwords

2. Click on the "Tools" menu on the home page the go down and click on "Keyword Planner"

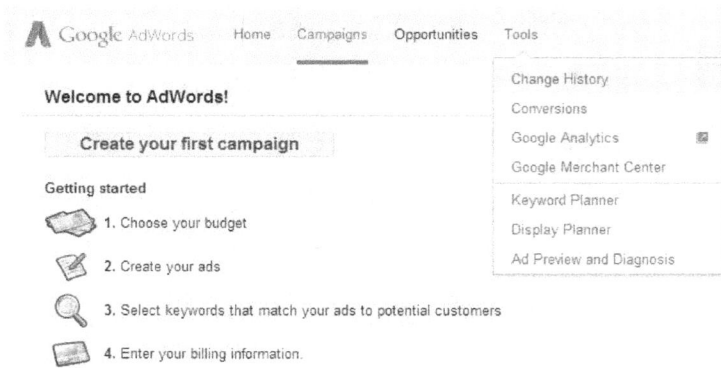

3. Click to search for a new keyword and ad group ideas

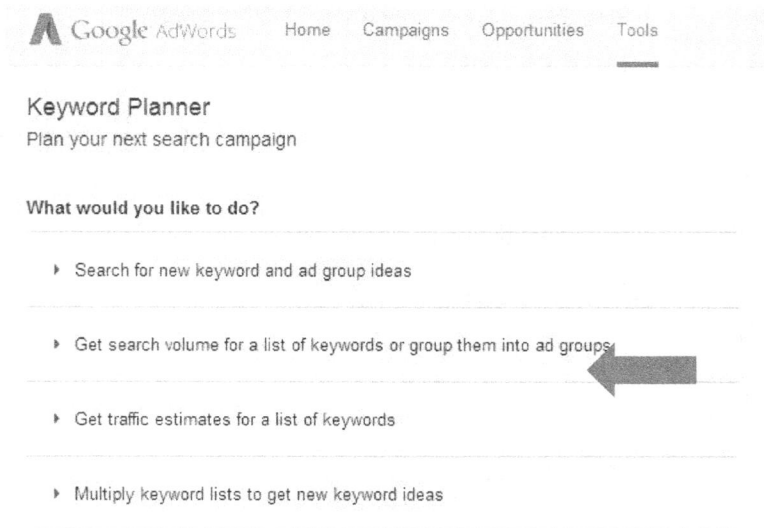

Figure 1-3

4. Type in some information to get started

▾ Search for new keyword and ad group ideas

Enter one or more of the following:

Your product or service

> For example, flowers or used cars

Your landing page

> www.example.com/page

Your product category

> Enter or select a product category ▾

Targeting ?   Customize your search ?

All locations   **Keyword filters**

All languages   **Keyword options**

Google   Show broadly related ideas

Negative keywords   Hide keywords in my account
                                     Hide keywords in my plan

                                     Include/Exclude

Get ideas

You can use this box to start your research. Since you are looking for keywords, you should let the tool give you some ideas. You can search by the specific product you're interested in selling, your company landing page or your product category.

This is what a keyword search would look like in the keyword planner. You can see some suggested keywords based on what you typed in as well as the value of those words and the average monthly searches. As you can see, a keyword doesn't need to have a lot of average monthly searches to be considered valuable.

I want to draw your attention to something you should make sure to check before you do your search. If you look at the section under "Targeting", you will notice that it says United States and English. A typical search will say "all" in those slots which means you'd be considering keywords all around the world in all languages. Since your business is based in the United States, you should focus on that area.

You could actually narrow it down further and focus only on your specific state. It's up to you but I suggest that you start broad first to get a good idea of what types of keywords are being used overall.

Now it's time to start choosing some words. You want to focus on the words that have the highest rank. Those will be the words with the most number of searches. You want your website to show up in as many searches as possible. Pick the top five keywords.

Once you've chosen the top five highest ranking keywords, use them with a geo modifier on the end. The geo modifier is the state or city where you r business is based. Using the picture in figure 1-5 as an example, you would choose "sell house fast Chicago" as your key phrase if your business was based in the Chicago area.

You don't want people looking for general information about selling their houses fast. You want people looking for information about selling their houses fast in Chicago. That will increase the odds that your business will show up over someone else's.

Here are examples of some of the top keywords focused on buying and selling houses:
- We buy houses
- Tips on selling your house
- Selling my house fast
- Buy my home
- Sell my house today

These are just examples. If you like these words, you should still use the tool to gain some additional ideas of words that would work best for your particular business.

Now you have some viable keywords that you know people are searching for to put in the content you're sharing on your website. And to top it all off, you were able to get this valuable information for free.

But in addition to all of this wonderful free insight with the keyword planner, Google has another great tool that can help your website rank well in searches, especially location specific ones.

Google Places

Google finds value in being considered a resource which is why the company works so hard to ensure that search results are high quality and relevant. Google Places is another tool that was created to provide even more value especially through the Google Maps tool.

Not only do people use Google to search general topics and information, they also search for more location specific things as well. This is especially applicable when they're searching for products and services. If you want to find an Italian restaurant for dinner, you won't be interested in websites from restaurants in California if you live in Michigan.

Google understands this and has worked to make the searches much more location oriented but they have gone a step further and found a way to allow business owners the opportunity to benefit from yet another tool. Google Places is that tool and it's free to list your business.

Once you've added your business, it will come up in searches that take place on the main Google search as well as on Google mobile and Google Maps. Plus, you can add more information to the listing to make it as valuable and robust as possible for visitors. Here is how you can make the most of your Google Places profile.

1. Use an address from the UPS Store or a PO Box but call it a suite.

   This will prevent people from showing up to your office and help you control the way leads come in.

2. Add as much business information as possible. Provide more than one form of contact like email address and phone number rather than just an email address or just a phone number. Make sure there is a link to your company website as well as a keyword rich description of your business.

3. Include 10 pictures

   Make sure you take advantage of the opportunity to feature pictures on your Google Places profile. You can share up to 10 so you should use them all.

4. Encourage customers to leave reviews

   It is possible for customers to leave reviews on your Google Places profile. You should encourage it because it adds more value to your profile.

Google Places is a great free tool that will help your business rank in another way in Google search results. When someone does a search, it doesn't just pull up Google Ads and general search engine results. It also pulls up local businesses that fit whichever keyword is being searched.

These local businesses are found based on where you're doing the search.
When you create a Google Places account, you make it possible for your business to show up in the Maps section of search results as well.

Businesses that have a Google Places account can get anywhere from 10-15 new customers a week from those listings alone. On top of it all, it's completely free to use.

Google has created two tools that are completely free and will help drive more business to your website and ultimately your business. There is, however, one other tool that is paid but can be very affordable.

Pay Per Click (PPC)

Like I said in the beginning of this chapter, Google Adwords was created to allow business owners to run ads on different Google websites. Pay Per Click (PPC) is the paid advertising portion of Google Adwords that any business owner can use. Since you've already created an account on Google Adwords, you can login and create your PPC campaign.

You can create a campaign with a text based ad, which is a short call to action with a link that people can click on if they're interested in learning more about your company. You can also create a campaign with a visual ad, which is an image combined with text and a link that people can click on. Once you've decided which type of ad you want to run, you set your budget then create your campaign.

PPC campaigns are keyword based so you would still use the keywords you identified previously. Once your ad starts to run, you pay when someone clicks on it. Once your budget runs out, the ad stops running. It's pretty simple and affordable. Your budget can be as big or as small as you want.

Since you have paid for the space, your ad will rank well for your particular keyword.

When you combine all three of Google's metrics: organic search results, Google Places and PPC, you have three different opportunities for your website to show up in search results. If you use all three of these tools, you could dominate Google for your particular keyword.

42% of people will do business with the top three results in Google and 5% of people will do business with companies that show up in Google Ads. That's a good percentage of people that are more likely to do business with you after seeing your website show up in a Google search with the bulk of them coming from something that's completely free to use.

Google is a tool that you have to take advantage of if you want to reach as many people as possible. It's where your customer spends a lot of his/her time. It's also where your customer goes first to learn about any company they may be considering doing business with.

As soon as a potential customer finds out who you are, they will go to the web to learn more about you. Those same customers are also much more likely to start the buying process online. In fact, 90% of prospects will start with an online search first.

If your business isn't easily found online, your customers may not take your business seriously. You have to take advantage of people's propensity towards doing a Google search by using search engine optimization (SEO) and search engine marketing (SEM) to make sure your business is all over those search results.

Search Engine Optimization

Search engine optimization (SEO) is when you use keywords on your website to help it show up organically in search results. You are essentially optimizing your website to make sure it ranks well in Google. There are some important things you must keep in mind when doing a SEO campaign.

1. It takes time.

   Since you are working to affect how your website ranks in organic search results, it will take time for your website to consistently show up on the first page of Google. While it doesn't take as long as it used to, you still have to give it time. It's tough to rush this process. But if you're doing everything I outlined in this chapter, your page will be well ranked in no time.

2. Avoid stuffing your website with keywords

   You shouldn't have more than 2.5 to 3.5% keywords on your website. It's not a good idea to repeat the same keyword multiple times within the content of your website.

Google will penalize your website if you do that so be conservative with the number of keywords that you use.

Search Engine Marketing

Search engine marketing (SEM) is when you optimize your social media websites to rank well for your keywords. Your social media profiles should all point to your website in some way. If it ranks well for your keyword that will help your business as well.

The key is to do everything in your power to make sure that your company name is showing up in as many searches as possible. Many social media websites tend to be better ranked than your own website so you should take advantage of that while your organic search results are working in your favor.

In addition to using Google specifically, there are other things you can do to help your website rank well.

Online Customer Reviews

I mentioned encouraging your customers to submit reviews on your Google Places profile because it's a valuable marketing tool. There are other review websites you can use for your business as well. Websites like Yelp, Angie's List, Yahoo Local and CitySearch are popular review websites. If you have the tech expertise or access to someone who can create a website, you can also make your own review website and encourage customers to leave reviews on it.

If you aren't already, you should really be taking advantage of these review websites. 60% of potential customers will search for reviews on your business before becoming a customer. However, you will have to do some reputation management when you start encouraging people to leave reviews.

Unfortunately, unhappy customers are 10 times more likely to leave a review than happy customers. You should make it a point to encourage customers to leave a review when you've done something wonderful for them. You could also help manage any potential negative reviews by encouraging those unhappy customers to leave them on the contact form for your website.

This way you can keep those reviews on file without them going public. You can then encourage those happy customers to leave positive reviews on the sites I mentioned previously like Yelp, Angie's List, Yahoo Local, CitySearch and Google Places.

Ultimately you really need to put a plan in place for how you want to handle reviews. You can encourage people to leave them by offering a coupon or discount.

Did You Enjoy Your Service?

We Want To Know
What You Think!

Tell Us How You Feel:

I am happy with the service :)

OR

I am unhappy with the service :(

Receive A Free Coupon for
voicing your opinion!

Figure 1-6

Figure 1-6 is a great example of a coupon you can share on your website to encourage reviews. You can link "I am happy with the service ☺" to one of the larger review websites and link "I am unhappy with the service ☹" to your company email address or contact form. It gives you the opportunity to benefit from sharing the positive reviews online while allowing you to turn those unhappy customers into happy ones by addressing their needs.

Often unhappy customers can be easily turned around by simply addressing the grievance head on. Then those customers often go on to leave glowing reviews about how you handled their issue with grace and care.

Use Backlinks

When other websites link to yours, it benefits your website by showing that other people consider it an authority resource. It can take time to build a network of organic backlinks but you can use social media websites to start getting backlinks to your website. You can share the link for your website on Facebook, Twitter, LinkedIn and BiggerPockets to benefit from the link juice from those very well ranked websites.

Ideally you will work on getting backlinks from websites with a page rank of 5 and over. The page rank is a system created to show how much of an authority a website is based on the websites that link to it. The higher the page rank, the more authoritative the website is. The page rank scale is from 1 to 10 but there are only a small number of really well ranked websites with a page rank of 7-10.

You can expect a website like Twitter, with a page rank of 10 and Facebook, with a page rank of 9, to have really high page ranks because a lot of people link to those websites. However, if a website has a page rank of 5 or 6, that's still very valuable for your Google rank.

This is a great way to boost your website in Google search so that you rank better than your competition. When you share those links to your website, you should make sure they are a combination of general links to the main domain and deeper links to specific pages on your website. If you have a blog and share links to specific blog posts, that's one way to do it.

Spy on Your Competition

I realize I've mentioned outranking your competition a few times. This is one way that many internet marketers create a plan to improve their Google rankings. They find out where their competitors rank and figure out what they're doing to have that rank. Then they work to do better than their competitors so they outrank them.

This is a common practice, and there are many tools out there that you can use to see what your competition is doing. One of them is free and it's called Follow. It gives you great insight into what your competitors are doing online and how they're making money in the process. Not only does this show you what your competitors are doing, it can also give you some ideas for strategies and tactics you may not have considered.

Follow is a browser extension that works for free on Chrome, Firefox and Safari web browsers. If you're using Internet Explorer, you should download one of these browsers and take advantage of it. You can download all of these browsers on either your Mac or PC computer for free.

Once you've downloaded it, you can use it to check for various things:

- View competitors' keywords to see their position on Google
- Follow competitors' social media practices to see what you could possibly do differently or better
- Review your competitors' online marketing strategies
- See what works and what doesn't work for your competitors

Follow also allows you to see what types of searches people are doing to find your competitors. You can review their broad searches or precise searches. Precise searches happen when someone puts quotation marks around the term they're searching.

This makes the search engine look only for that exact particular word or phrase as it is. When you do a broad search, you don't put quotation marks around the word or phrase. The search engine looks for that particular word or phrase as well as instances that may be related but not exact. You tend to get more diverse results using a broad search.

This type of information can be invaluable in mapping out how you are going to effectively dominate Google and make your website as visible as possible. It's so much better to work smart rather than hard. There's no reason you should be racking your brain for a Google strategy when you can go out and use someone else's as inspiration and do it better.

Whew!

I know I just gave you a LOT of information to digest about Google. Take your time and re-read it until you understand it thoroughly. You should explore the different tools I've mentioned and get acquainted with them. Dominating Google is one of the backbones of internet marketing. Once you've done it a few times, you will find that it becomes much easier and more seamless.

One more thing you need to keep in mind is variety in your marketing tactics. I know it may seem easier to choose one tactic and stick with it, especially when it works. Don't do that. Variety is the spice of life when it comes to internet marketing. If you stick to one tactic, it will eventually stop working as well.

Remember this chapter is about you **dominating** Google, not just making your presence known on Google. Use at least FOUR different marketing strategies a month. Switch it up to ensure that you continue to dominate.

Chapter 2: Cracking the Facebook Code

Now that we've tackled the largest search engine in the world, it's time to tackle the largest social media website in the world.

Did you know that if Facebook were a country it would be the third largest country in the world, behind China?

Facebook has more users than many countries has citizens. If you aren't using Facebook to boost your business, you are leaving a LOT of money on the table. Plus, it's completely free to use many of the features that Facebook offers.

Let's get into it.

The main thing you need to understand about Facebook is that it is made up of profiles and pages. Everyone has to create a profile to use Facebook. Profiles are the personal side of Facebook and must be created by a human. You have to input your personal information initially to go through the process of setting it up. But once it's set up, you can hide things like your age, birthday, name, phone number, etc.

However, you can't skip that part. If you don't have a Facebook profile, go ahead and set it up. It will immediately open you up to the different features and benefits of using Facebook.

Once your profile is set up, you are able to create a Facebook Fan Page for your business. The fan page is essentially a profile for a business, brand or organization. The difference between the profile and the page is how they're used.

Fan pages can be anonymous but they are a separate identity from your personal profile even though pages have to be connected to a profile. Fan pages also have less ability to interact with people on Facebook. Unlike with profiles where you can go out and invite people to be your friend and have them accept your friend request before you can interact with them, people can just like your page and you can interact with them.

Just like with Google and any other tool you use for your business, there has to be a strategy when you use Facebook.

Facebook Strategy

Before you dive in and create your fan page, you need to come up with a plan for making sure the page stays active and consistently updated.

Take some time and create 10-15 posts that you will share on your fan page once it's created. You need to do this BEFORE your page is live and viewable by the public. There's nothing worse than having a fan page set up with only sad little post and nothing else.

Once you've created those initial posts that will be shared on your fan page as soon as it's live, create 10 more that you will post over the next couple of months. You can start by updating your page once or twice a week and increase the consistency from there. The idea is to get your page up and moving right away while it's still fresh and new.

If you need help determining the kinds of posts, you should start by deciding what the purpose of your fan page will be.

1. Brand building

   Are you using this page to establish your brand and use social media to do it? If so, you should create content focused on educating people about your company, who you are and why you exist.

2. List building

   Do you want to build an email marketing list for your business? If so, you should create content designed to encourage people to sign up for more information. It will be teaser or informational content that entices readers to want to know more. Then you can send those readers links to your email sign up page or include that option on your fan page directly.

3. Direct sales

Are you trying to increase your sales? If so, you should create content that highlights your products/services and shares customer testimonials and positive experiences with your business.

Usually it's a combination of all three of these purposes, but it helps to focus on one at a time. As you can see, each one has a different strategy if you want to maximize the results. Once you've identified your purpose, it will help you decide which type of page you will have. There are three different types of pages:

1. Branding Site

This site will share a lot of information about your company and the different things that you do. Make sure you don't share too much information and confuse people about the purpose of your page.

2. Landing Page

This type of page will have a very specific focus and call to action for people to follow.

3. Gravity Site

This type of site is focused on creating leads for your business. It may focus on one specific idea or concept and may act as a forum for your business.

One thing to keep in mind is that while your page can address all three purposes and feature all three page types, it's best to start with one and build from there. You want to work on building your page with a clear focus before expanding. If you try to do too many things at one time, you run the risk of confusing yourself and your fans.

Now that you've determined the purpose of your page and what type of page you may want it to be, you're ready to set it up.

1. Go to www.facebook.com/pages and click "Create Page" to get started.

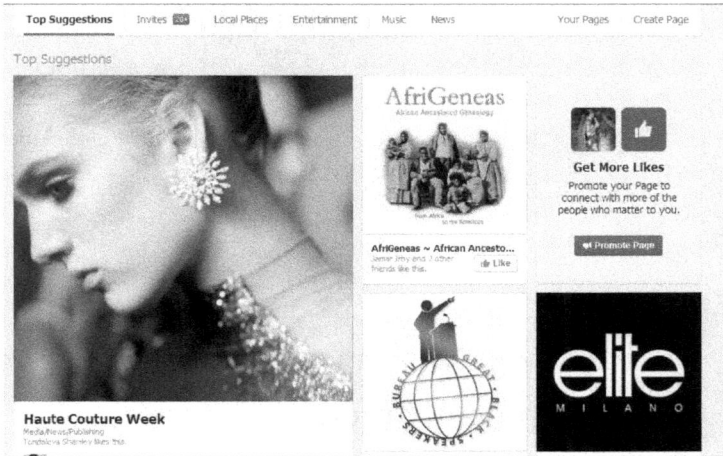

Your fan page may look a bit different because it will be a combination of pages that people in your network have already liked. However, this is the general layout.

2. Choose the kind of page you will have.

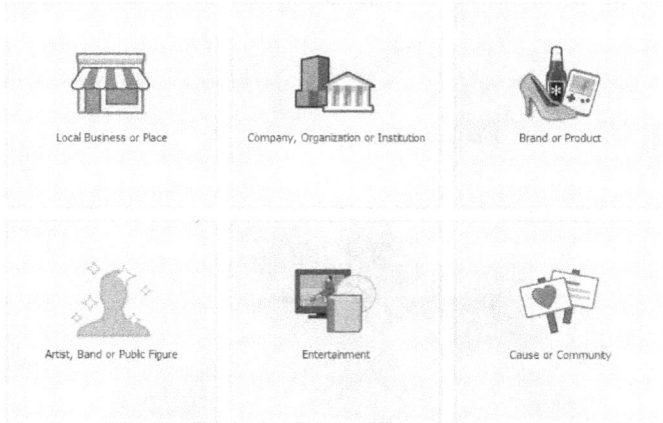

Local Business or Place Company, Organization or Institution Brand or Product

Artist, Band or Public Figure Entertainment Cause or Community

Choose wisely. You want to make sure your page is properly represented from the beginning.

3. Input your business information. Fill out every field. The more information you provide, the better.

Local Business or Place

Choose a category	▼

Business or Place Name

Street Address

City/State

Zip Code

Phone

☐ I agree to Facebook Pages Terms

Get Started

4. Fill in a description of your company and make sure you include one or two of your keywords. Include what category your business is in, a link to your website and a unique Facebook web address. As you can see, you can't change that address so choose wisely.

Set Up Test Business

| 1 About | 2 Profile Picture | 3 Reach More People |

Add categories, a description and a website to improve the ranking of your Page in search.
Fields marked by asterisks (*) are required

*Category (ex. Chinese restaurant, museum)

*Add a description with basic info for Test Business.

Website (ex: your website, Twitter or Yelp links)   Add Another Site

Choose a unique Facebook web address to make it easier for people to find your Page. Once this is set, it can't be changed.
http://www.facebook.com/ Enter an address for your Page ...

Is Test Business a real establishment, business or venue?   ○ Yes ○ No
This will help people find this establishment, business or venue more easily on Facebook.

Visit Help Center   **Save Info**

5. Upload your profile picture. It can either be a picture of you or your company logo. Make sure it's a good, clear picture that shows the entire image.

Now that your page is up and ready, it's time for you to optimize it. Before you make it live, you should make some edits to it. You want your page to be fully developed before you share it with the world. Remember, this is another reflection of your brand. If it's half done, it will reflect poorly on your business.

Here are some things you should do to optimize your page:

1. Upload a cover photo that describes your business. It should contain your contact information and one or two of your keywords.

2. You should have uploaded your profile photo in the setup process but you should make sure that it is a good quality photo that either clearly displays your logo or face.

3. The tabs are the different sections of your page. The tabs on your page can be things like photos, videos, articles and opt-in forms. This is an area of your page where you can look for ways to provide additional value and information for your visitors. The more value they see in your page, the more likely they are to like it.

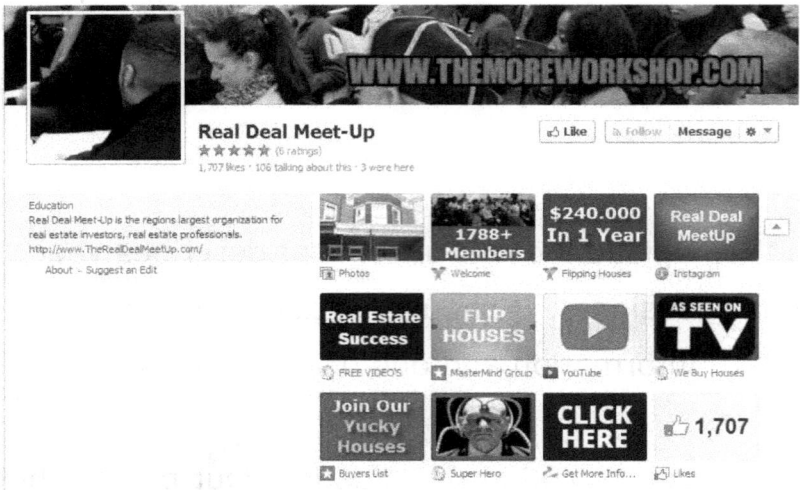

4. Make sure your images and pictures are the right size. Your images should be of good quality. It's not a good idea to take the time and upload some great pictures only to realize that they're too small and look really pixelated and unclear. Below is a figure that shows the ideal sizes for pictures on Facebook.

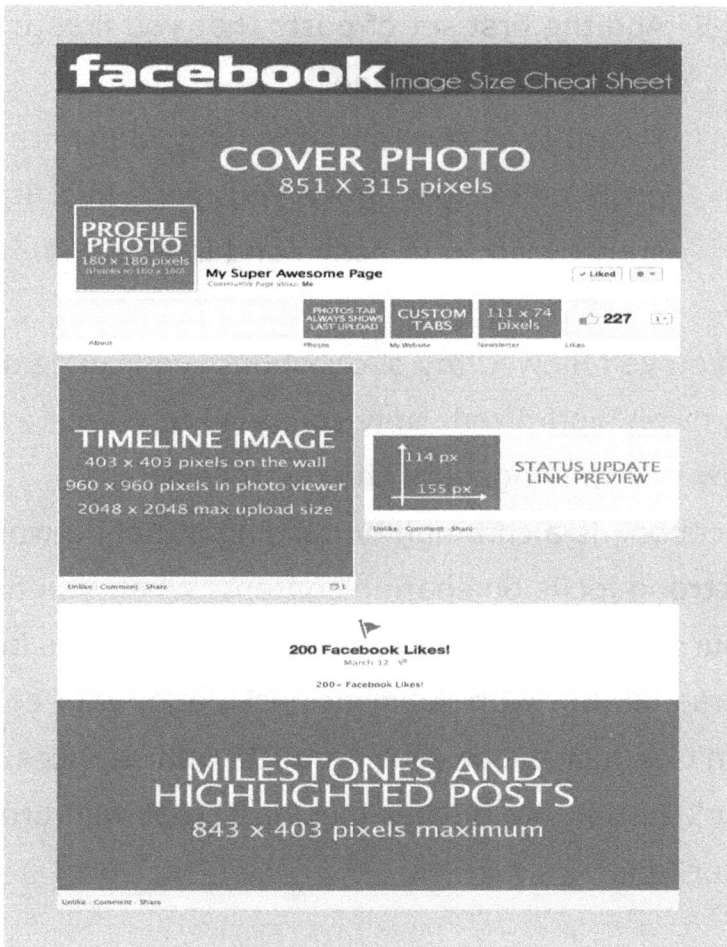

When you upload any pictures or images, keep in mind that they're going to be resized to fit these particular dimensions.

5. Add the first set of posts that you created before setting up your page.

I want to reiterate that you should share those posts before you make your page live. It should start out looking active and interesting.

If you've followed my suggestions, your page should be nicely optimized. Now you need to create a plan for how you will engage with your followers.

Facebook is a community building social network with a strong focus on sharing content. When you have your personal page, the content you share is largely personal. But with your business page, your content can't be just about your products and services. You can't turn it into a sales machine. That will turn off your fans.

You have to look for a way to provide value and share information that will be considered beneficial. Then you can infuse the content about your business in with the other information you're sharing. Put yourself in your customer's shoes. Think of the kind of information they may want to read.

In addition to sharing business related content, you should also share content that is funny and entertaining. That will help personalize your page and let your fans know that there is a person behind it. You're not just a faceless business.

Here are two pages you can use to find funny viral videos and pictures to share on your page.

- Amazing Crazy Videos
- Beautiful & Amazing Photo Collection

You can use the content on these pages and share it on yours. There are lots of funny, cute and interesting photos and videos that go viral online. These videos help with personalizing your page. People like working with the people running the business, not just the business.

As I mentioned, you should also be including business related content with the viral and informative content that you're sharing. Here are some types of posts you could share that relate to your business:

- Deals/Sales
- Benefits of your services
- Free bonuses
- Contest/Giveaways

The purpose of these and all of your other posts should be to sell yourself but in a way that isn't overly aggressive and pushy. Your page is there to build a community of leads that will support your business because you've taken the time to build a connection with them through your page.

After you've figured out what you plan to post, it's important to know when to post. Although the Facebook community is on it at all times of the day, there are times when it's most ideal to post content. These are times when people are most apt to be online.

- Morning: 6am to 9am
- Afternoon: 11am to 1pm
- Evening: 5pm to 7pm

If you want to get your posts in front of the most people, share new content during these times.

Timeline Story

The feed that features the different posts you share is called the Facebook timeline. When you create your page, you can use this as a way to further tell the story of your business. You already have a plan for how often you'll be posting and the type of content you'll be sharing. You can also add milestones that have been reached by your business.

This allows you to show people your business journey even though your page is new. You want to demonstrate that you are an established business and this is a great way to do it. When you add milestones, include information about when you opened, when you added products and services, customer milestones you may have reached and other successes you've experienced. It will show your fans that you have a track record of success.

Even if your business has only been around a short amount of time, you can still highlight your successes and milestones. It will help establish you as an expert which is another valuable benefit of having a Facebook page.

Facebook Ads

Just like with Google PPC ads, Facebook also has an advertising component. It is very budget friendly because you can decide how much you want to spend and let your ad run until your budget runs out. You pay when someone clicks on your ad and interacts with it in some way. An ideal click rate is 1%.

There are a few different types of ads that you can use to encourage engagement. Each ad type also includes layout suggestions you can use when creating these types of ads.

1. Like Ad

This is an ad designed to encourage someone to like your page and become a fan. Below is an example of a Like Ad.

Title (25 characters)
Links to Page on Facebook
Title should match the name of Page

Image or Video Thumbnail
(110x80 px)
Links to Page on Facebook

Like
people like [your brand]

Ben & Jerry's

Every flavor creation is a tongue-teasing treat. So what are you waiting for? Grab your favorite pint and fill your life with yum!

Body Copy
(135 characters)

1,749,031 people like Ben & Jerry's.

Like

2. Poll Engagement Ad

This is an ad that works to engage people with a short poll. Below is an example of a Poll Engagement Ad.

Title (25 characters)
Links to Page on Facebook
or client specified URL

Image or Video Thumbnail
(110x80 px)
Links to Page on Facebook
or client specified URL

Question (40 characters)

Responses (25 characters)
2 or 3 choices

Toy Story 3

Buzz, Woody and the gang are back in this summer's great escape! In UK cinemas now in Disney Digital 3D and IMAX 3D.

Body Copy
(135 characters)

How excited are you to see Toy Story 3?
○ Excited
○ Very excited
○ Buzzing!

3. Event Ad

This is an ad designed to encourage people to RSVP for and ultimately attend an event. Below is an example of an Event Ad.

4. Video Comment Ad

This is an ad that is designed to encourage people to watch and comment on a video. Below is an example of a Video Comment Ad.

5. Marketplace Ad

   Facebook has a marketplace where members can advertise different products and services. These ads are free because you don't have as much control over who sees them or when. But that doesn't make it any less valuable. It's still beneficial to use them especially since it's free. Below is an example of some Marketplace Ads.

How to create a marketplace ad:

a. Visit

www.facebook.com/marketplace

and click the post button

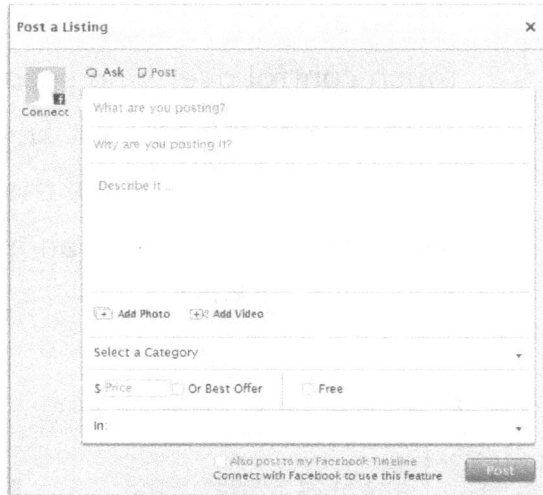

Fill in the above box. Make sure you connect it to Facebook because the marketplace is run by an app called oodle. Once you've filled in the information, click post and your post will be in the marketplace. Make sure you click on the arrows in the "Select a Category" and "In:" sections to provide that information. If you have pictures and video, include it. You can post up to 8 pictures in your ad. Your ad will run for 30 days.

6. Sponsored Stories Ad

This is an ad that creates a story about what other people in your network have done. Below is an example of a Sponsored Story Ad.

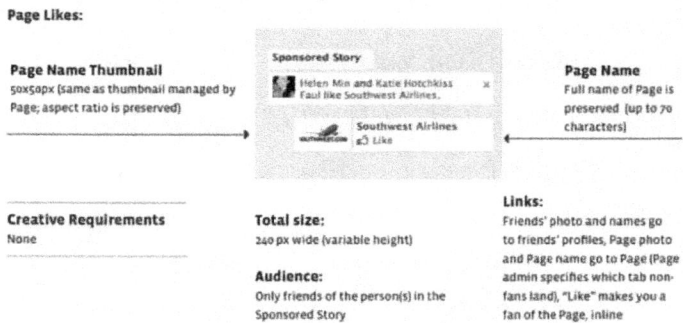

Page Likes:

Page Name Thumbnail 50x50px (same as thumbnail managed by Page; aspect ratio is preserved)	Sponsored Story Helen Min and Katie Hotchkiss Faul like Southwest Airlines. x Southwest Airlines Like	**Page Name** Full name of Page is preserved (up to 70 characters)
Creative Requirements None	**Total size:** 240 px wide (variable height) **Audience:** Only friends of the person(s) in the Sponsored Story	**Links:** Friends' photo and names go to friends' profiles, Page photo and Page name go to Page (Page admin specifies which tab non-fans land), "Like" makes you a fan of the Page, inline

As you can see, there are several types of ads you can run on Facebook. You should decide what you'd like to accomplish then find the ad that supports that goal. You can run more than one type of ad but it's best to start with one type of ad and see how it does before running multiple types of ads. You want to get some insight into the process to see how it all works.

Facebook has a lot of great metrics information that will tell you how much engagement your ad got and from whom. You can gain a lot of great insight from running an ad on Facebook. When you're ready to set up an ad, visit www.facebook.com/advertising.

Facebook is a great tool for increasing your business while building an active community at the same time. Yes there are some paid features but the majority of it is totally free. As a business owner, I know you can appreciate any opportunity to use a free tool that's going to work on your behalf.

But one important thing you have to remember is engagement. Not only do you want people to engage and interact with your page, you also want to make sure you engage and interact with those people. Like I said before, Facebook requires you to show that there is a person behind your company. People don't just send out messages without responding in kind.

Facebook has different measurements and algorithms in place to encourage engagement from members. When owners of pages, take the time to truly interact with fans, they benefit from having good edgerank. Edgerank essentially measures your authority on Facebook. The more you interact with the people on your page in a timely and meaningful manner, the higher your edgerank.

I know you may not think you have time to be on social media sharing posts about what you had for dinner or what you're doing this weekend. This isn't the only thing Facebook is about. Now that you have all of this wonderful insight into the value of Facebook, you should start taking advantage of it.

Chapter 3: Optimizing Your Success with Wordpress

Wordpress is a content management system that's pretty popular because it's very easy to use and is free. It's also very robust and can be used to create a variety of websites. Because Wordpress is so popular, there are lots of different tools out there to further optimize any website that uses it. There are also a lot of free tools that will help you use it effectively.

It's very important that you have the ability to update your website and manage the content that you share. Wordpress allows you to do that even if you hire a professional to design the way it looks. But this chapter is going to be about some of the strategies, tactics and tools you can be using to get the most out of your website.

Above the Fold

Remember when I mentioned things being "above the fold" on your website? Well now I'm going to go into more detail about what you should be putting "above the fold".

So let me give you a quick refresher on what it means for something to be "above the fold". Essentially, it's any part of your website that appears before anyone has to scroll down. This is valuable real estate that you should take full advantage of. Here are the things you need to make sure to have "above the fold" on your website.

Calls to Action

There needs to be multiple calls to action on your website "above the fold". You want to encourage people to do something on your website as soon as the page comes up. Here are some examples of the different calls to action you should feature:

- Video telling visitors to do something
  Videos are great tools for communicating with visitors to your website. If you have a

video towards the top of your website, it should be directive and tell people to do something like join the email list, sign up for a workshop, call for a quote, etc.

- Links to free quotes
  If you offer free quotes, it's important that you tell people about it right away. Don't make them look for free information or services. Make it prominent.

- Telephone number
  Make it easy for people to see how to contact you. Many websites list the phone number at the very bottom of the page. Don't do this. Put it at the top in large font.

- Contact information form
  Contact forms are often hidden somewhere on the website. Don't make people work really hard to find your contact information. Put the form somewhere it can be easily seen and

accessed.

- Opt-in form

  If you have an email list (and you should), ask people to leave their email address as soon as they visit your website. If you put this form towards the bottom or on another page, you run the risk of them not seeing it.

- Social media icons

  If you want people to know that you have social media profiles, make that known up front and right away. Don't bury those icons on other pages or below the fold.

- Call tracking number

  If you want to track the customers that contact you, you can use a call tracking number to keep up with that information. Rather than including your office phone number, you can use a call tracking number to gather valuable statistics about people contacting your business. It can show you if your website is effectively generating leads or not.

When you want visitors to your website to do something, you should make it a point to do that up front. You can have as many of these calls to action as can fit without cluttering the website.

This is the main page of one of my websites. Notice how the page isn't cluttered but is still asking visitors to do several different things. There is a phone number, a contact form, free quotes and video. It is possible to make the most of your space "above the fold" so you should definitely do it.

Landing Page

A landing page is an invaluable tool for building your email list or encouraging visitors to become customers. The great thing about a landing page is that its purpose is to ask visitors to do something. They can be used to ask them to make a purchase or leave their email address.

Essentially landing pages gives visitors to your website two choices: do business with my company or leave the website. It's very clear and doesn't come off as pushy in any way.

Below are two tools you can use to create effective landing pages:

InstaBuilder

This is a Wordpress plugin you can use to optimize your website for marketing. It allows you to easily create a landing page or squeeze page designed to get conversions of some kind. In fact, when you go to the website, you can see the kind of sales page that could be created.

LeadPages

This is a tool that helps you create landing pages, sales pages and any other type of conversion page.

Landing pages allow you to clearly identify the problem that you're solving, show how you will solve it and encourage visitors to get involved with your solution. Every business should be taking advantage of targeted landing pages.

Chapter 4: YouTube Video Marketing Success

YouTube is a free video distribution platform that is owned by Google. This is very important and one thing that really separates YouTube from other video distribution platforms. I know I've mentioned a few times that video is a great way to talk to your audience through your website and on social media. One of the challenges of sharing video is figuring out where to host it.

It can be expensive and challenging to put video on your own web hosting server. Video files can be very large but that doesn't mean you shouldn't use it. Video distribution websites like YouTube make it possible for people to easily upload and share videos. But in addition to being a great tool for hosting your videos, YouTube is also a marketing powerhouse.

When you do a Google search, you have the option of looking specifically for videos about whatever it is that you're searching for. But those videos also may come up in the organic search results as well. This makes sharing videos on YouTube very valuable for driving traffic to your website and helping you rank high in search engine results.

Even if you are only using YouTube to share videos on your website or social media profiles, you should still take the time to optimize those videos and organize your YouTube channel.

Here are the different areas you should focus on optimizing on YouTube:

- Channel Name
  Make sure the name of your YouTube channel has a keyword followed by the name of your state in it.

- Title
  Whenever you upload a video, the title of it should have one of your keywords in it.

- Descriptions

  You should take full advantage of the video description and make sure to include at least three of your keywords in it. Make sure you include a link to your website in the description box to encourage people to visit your website with every video you post.

- Tags

  This is the section that allows you to essentially stuff your video posts with keywords. You want to use several of your keywords to describe your video. These will definitely be keywords that will help people find your video.

- Retargeting: When your ad follows the viewer all over the internet

  This is a practice that happens when you run a pay per click campaign and your ad follows visitors to your website all over Google.

Let me show you how to set up your YouTube Channel properly:

1. This is what it will look like when you upload a video:

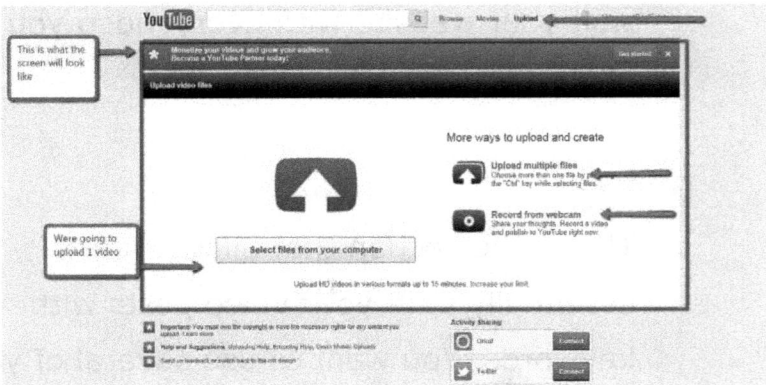

2. This is the info section for your video. Once it's been uploaded, you should fill in this information making sure to use keywords. You will have to do this for every video.

3. This is the info section of your channel. Don't forget to fill in this information with a keyword rich title, description and tags.

You will only have to fill in the channel settings once so make sure you use the most valuable keywords and that your description really brands your business.

This is what people will see when they visit your YouTube Channel so make the most of it.

The great thing about YouTube is that it's a Google product so you get immediate access to Google search when you post a video. This is one of the easiest ways to have your business show up higher in search results because video is so valuable.

The most important thing is to focus on creating high quality video content that educates viewers in some way. You're not creating these videos to become the next YouTube star. You're creating them to drive traffic and sales to your website.

I know some of you may be hesitant to record videos because you don't feel that you will be good on camera. It's important to remember a few facts about YouTube videos:

- The average video on YouTube is 5 minutes long.
- 70% percent of your viewers will remain for 30 seconds.

- 50% of your viewers will remain after 60 seconds.
- Only 25% of your viewers will stay around after 2 minutes.

When you consider these statistics, you should consider that your video doesn't have to be very long. In fact, it should probably be much closer to two minutes than five. So think about that. Your face doesn't have to be on the screen more than a couple of minutes. I think you can handle being on video for that long. Plus, if you focus on the value you're providing, it will make things so much less painful for you.

Besides, when you consider how much exposure video can give to your business in Google and overall, you should take a deep breath and make those videos. Now if you're worrying about whether you can afford to hire someone to create those videos, you don't. You can use Animoto to easily create great looking videos that you can feature on your YouTube Channel.

Animoto has both free and paid plans but the free plan only lets you do 30 second videos. However, if you get the $5 a month plan, you can do videos up to 10 minutes long but they will still have the Animoto brand on them. If you want to remove their branding, it will cost $39 a month.

So you don't have to go out and hire someone to make your videos right away. As you do more, you may decide to go that route but you can get started using Animoto.

Additional YouTube Tips

Once you've gotten your YouTube Channel set up with your keywords and description, you should also do some things to get more traction for your channel.

1. Create a video creation plan.
   You want to create good quality videos consistently which means you should take some time to plan the different topics you want to cover and how often you will record them. Approach this like you did your Facebook page

content plan. Think of some things your customers want to know and talk about them. You should also include a request for people to ask questions or suggest topics they'd like you to cover. It's a great way to engage your audience.

2. Make sure your videos aren't too long. Remember that only 25% of the people that watch your video will stick around after two minutes. If you keep your videos under two minutes, you can say what you need to say before you lose people.

3. Comment and like other people's videos. Find other YouTube Channels with high traffic and a lot of videos and get involved in their community. Like and comment on their videos. If any of them ask for video responses, you could make your video a response to theirs. It's a great way to tie your channel into one that has more engagement while benefitting from some great exposure.

4. Look for trend topics you can focus on in your videos.

   Visit the YouTube Trends Dashboard and see what's currently trending. See if there's a way for you to take advantage of a trend in your videos.

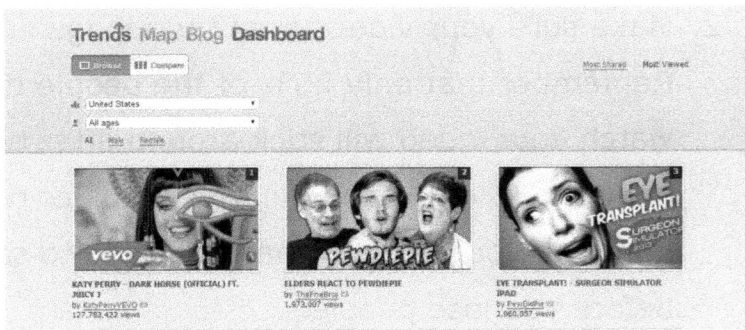

5. Take advantage of the tags feature.

   You should use as many of your keywords as often as possible when you're posting videos. This is a great way to make sure your videos show up in search engine results. You can't use keyword stuffing on your website but that doesn't apply to YouTube.

6. Create a video ad.

If you've ever watched a video on YouTube, you may have noticed that there are short video commercials that will run before the content you're interested in starts. YouTube has now made it possible for businesses to take advantage of that space with video ads or commercials. While it is a part of Google Ads, it's a separate section because these ads will only run on YouTube. Visit www.youtube.com/yt/advertise to learn more and sign up.

By taking advantage of YouTube, you are contributing to you Google domination that I discussed in the first chapter. This will give you another opportunity for your business to show up in search results. As long as you are creating quality content and solving problems, you will really help drive lots of traffic to your website.

But one important thing to focus on is conversions with your YouTube videos, not how many viewers you get. As long as you're getting 20-25 people per 100 views responding to your call to action, then your videos are working well. Aim for a 20-25% conversion rate.

Using YouTube videos is a great way to showcase your expertise which will help sell your business without you having to actually sell it.

Chapter 5: Working with Virtual Assistants

You shouldn't try to do everything yourself but I know it can be expensive to go out and hire employees. Rather than trying to find it in your budget to hire someone or asking unqualified family members to help with your business, you should use virtual assistants and outsourcers.

Virtual assistants aren't just people who will do administrative tasks for your business. There are freelancers out there that will help with everything from designing and running your website to managing your business operations. You should always make it a point to hire people that are smarter than you.

Don't try to tackle tasks that don't contribute to the growth of your business. Your time is precious and you need to use it to increase your bottom line.

Online outsourcing, which includes virtual assistants, can be a very cost effective way to take some of those time consuming tasks off of your plate. Sometimes you can get so caught up in running your business that you don't spend any time shaping your business vision.

Before you take on a task, stop and ask yourself two questions:

- Do I currently have the skill set to complete the task I need done?
- Can someone else do the task cheaper than I can do it myself?

If you answer no to the first question and yes to the other one, you should look into online outsourcing. Here are some websites you can use to find and hire outsourcers:

- Guru
- Elance
- GetAFreelancer
- 99 Designs
- Odesk

- Freelancer

You can find people to do virtually anything you need on these websites. Before you hire someone, make sure you have a very specific task in mind. These websites have bidding systems where you post the job you need done and outsourcers create proposals for how they will complete the work.

You can choose the proposal you want to go with and start working with that person. If you are very specific about the task you need accomplished, you will get the most out of your outsourcing relationships.

Once you've started working with outsourcers and virtual assistants, you will need a way to coordinate with them. When you have remote employees, it's important to have a way to touch base and make sure they have what they need to complete the tasks and you can keep up with the projects they're working on. Here are some tools you can use to communicate with your outsourcers and virtual assistants:

- CallFire

This is a tool that allows you to communicate with multiple outsourcers via text. If you don't need to do a conference call but want to send an urgent update, text is a great route to go.

- **DropBox**

This is a tool you can use to store and share files online. It's a great way for sharing files in a team environment so everyone has one resource for any documents or other information you need to pass along.

- **Skype**

This is an online communication service. You can talk with people via text or phone. You can do group conference calls and text conversations as well. It's a pretty standard communication tool for outsourcers and other freelancers, even overseas. Since its web based, you can speak with outsourcers anywhere in the world.

- **Podio**

This is a tool that allows you to manage your business workflow. You can track your closing process, track your leads and build your buyers and sellers lists.

- **Asana**

  This is a tool that allows you to keep up with tasks and things that your team is working on. You can assign projects and check in to see where everyone is on the project timeline. It's a great way to keep up with what everyone is doing while holding them accountable to deadlines.

When you start using outsourcers, it's important that you plan to take full advantage of their assistance. You want to start by creating two separate workflows: selling houses and buying houses. Then you should plug in where each outsourcer fits into those workflows. You can use Podio to keep up with who's doing what and where they fit into your overall work plan.

Your main goal is to get out there and close those deals. You should always be closing deals which means you need to use outsourcers to do everything else. Like I said before, you should work smart not hard. Here are some things you should keep in mind when hiring outsourcers:

- Post jobs with the option to pay half upfront and the other half once the job is completed
- Hire people with a working knowledge of cold calling
- Give outsourcers scripts
- Hire a manager to manage your team and use group skype to stay in touch
- Set and keep deadlines
- Pay commissions rather than flat fees when possible

Although these outsourcers aren't your employees, you want to create an environment where there is a level of trust and integrity in how you work with them and how they work with you. If you plan and prepare for how you want people to help you, they can really help fill in any blanks you may have to address.

Never try to turn your business into a one man (or woman) show. Even if you can do something, it doesn't mean you should do it.

Chapter 6: Remember

You now have the tools you need to use internet marketing to create a steady stream of customers and increase your income considerably. I know I've given you a lot to think about and consider, so I'm going to summarize what I discussed.

The Big Four

You need to make sure you are taking full advantage of the four tools I just discussed in this book. I want to point out that all of these tools are largely free. Not only are they free, you are currently reading a book that tells you exactly how to use them for your business.

If you were on the fence about taking advantage of them before, I hope my book has helped moved you off of it and onto the positive side.

Google

Google is the largest search engine in the world. The first chapter explained how you can not only benefit from it but how you can dominate it. I have given you the tools to dominate the largest search engine in the world. Take advantage of them!

Facebook

Facebook is the largest social networking website in the world. It's a community of billions of members that are potential customers for your business. Like I said before, it's not just about going online and talking about your weekend plans or your niece's graduation. It's about building a business and making a considerable income.

Wordpress

Wordpress is a content management system that allows anyone to create and run their own website. It's easy to use and can help you optimize your website for optimal levels of success.

YouTube

Some people call YouTube one of the other largest search engines but it's not an official search engine. It's a HUGE database of videos with millions more being added on a regular basis. You have a plan you can use to make this database really work for your business. Plus, since it's owned by Google, it will help support your Google domination. It's a win-win!

You can use all four of these tools to actively market your business and gain new customers. I realize I've told you how to use these tools without outlining the different forms of marketing you can employ.

Forms of Marketing

Marketing is a diverse practice with a lot of ways you can use it to reach potential customers. Even when you're using the tools I've been discussing, it's important that you recognize those strategies and use them appropriately for maximum impact.

When you think of marketing strategies, you should look at it like a sphere of conversion. The easiest client to convert is the one that you're speaking to from a referral point of view.

- Word of Mouth Referrals
  These are the closest thing you can get to a warm lead. When someone tells another person to work with your business, they're much more likely to do so.

- Face to Face Cold Leads
  It can be tough to approach someone who doesn't know you and turn them into a customer but that doesn't make it any less effective. When you can look someone in the eye, it helps create a tangible connection.

- Telephone Calls
  Calls are much more effective when it's a warm lead than a cold one. But cold calling can still be very beneficial as long as you're working from a qualified lead.

- Direct Mail Marketing

People still enjoy receiving mail. Even though everything is electronic nowadays it doesn't mean that the good old post office isn't still a viable way to reach customers.

- Email Message Follow Up
Virtually everyone has email. If someone has visited your website, landing page, squeeze page or other online tool and left their email address, you should follow up fairly quickly. Although many people receive a lot of email, they are more apt to look for messages from people they want to receive information from. If they give you their email address, that signifies an interest.

- Text Message Blast
People live with their mobile phones at their sides. You can often reach someone via text quicker than with a phone call. If you text them some valuable information about your business, they will definitely receive it. When someone is interested in buying, selling or renting a

property, it's helpful to be able to reach them in as many ways as possible.

When you decide to launch a marketing campaign, it takes a 360 degree approach. You have to market to them from all sides and leave no stone unturned. Here are some more tools you can use to further enhance your marketing campaigns.

I like to call these the special sauce.

- **Social Lead Freak**

  Use this tool to build your leads list using Facebook and Google.

- **WooBox**

  This tool will help you create contests, sweepstakes, coupons and other promotions on your Facebook page.

- **Slydial**

  Use this tool to send voicemail messages to people relatively quickly and easily.

There you have it. You now have a treasure trove of tools you can use to guarantee the success of your business. I realize it's a lot of information. Go through each chapter and make sure you understand how each tool works.

Then start implementing! Success waits for no one!